walking backwards

WALKING backwards

NEW POEMS

Shirley Geok-lin Lim

WEST END PRESS

Some of these poems have appeared in the journals
*ARIEL, Awareness, Cha, Hedgebrook Journal, Mascara, Solo,
The Paterson Literary Review, Westerly,* and *Yuan Yang.*
Her work has also been included in the anthologies *Replacing
America; Tilting the Continent: An Anthology of Southeast Asian
American Writing; City Voices: Hong Kong Writing in English;
Poetry OutLoud; Petals of Hibiscus: A Representative Anthology
of Malaysian Literature in English; Across State Lines:
America's Fifty States as Represented in Poetry; Hong Kong
U Writing;* and *Language for a New Century: Contemporary
Poetry from the Middle East, Asia, and Beyond.*

First edition, October 2010
Paperback ISBN 978-0-9826968-0-4

Book design by Nancy Woodard
Front cover photograph by Steven Hirst

For book information, see our Web site at www.westendpress.org

West End Press
P.O. Box 27334
Albuquerque, NM 87125

Contents

Acknowledgments

Writers owe debts to a host of creditors, and this book particularly owes its existence to many generous hosts. First, I thank John Crawford, Nancy Woodard, and West End Press for their unwavering belief in the poems and support. My thanks to my life partner, Charles Bazerman. I am grateful to all the heroines whose works have served as foundation for my writing: Maxine Hong Kingston, Florence Howe, and Susan Gubar, to name only three out of a multitude. I am grateful for the residencies, fellowships, and visiting positions in many institutions that have provided the space and time for these poems to be written, in particular, the Fulbright Fellowships and State Department-sponsored visits to Singapore, Nepal, and Australia; Simmons Hall and the Department of Foreign Languages and Literatures, Massachusetts Institute of Technology; the Freeman Foundation and the Salzburg Seminar in American Studies; Hedgebrook at Whidbey Island; the University of Hong Kong and City University of Hong Kong; the Lock Up Cultural Centre and Hunter Writers Centre, Newcastle; and many other universities and centers in Austria, Germany, Spain, the United Kingdom, Canada, Australia, the People's Republic of China, Taiwan, Korea, and South-East Asia. My thanks to Dennis Haskell, University of Western Australia; Boey Kim Cheng, University of Newcastle, Kerrie Coles and Brian Joyce of the Lock Up Cultural Centre and Hunter Writers Centre; Page Richards, University of Hong Kong; Shreedhar Lohani, Tribhuvan University; Kingsley Bolton, City University of Hong Kong; Isabelle De Courtivron, Massachusetts Institute of Technology; and to the entire universe of scholars, cultural workers and writers who have offered me hospitality, friendship, and refuge. Their names, numerous and luminous, rival a galaxy of stars, and they will forgive me for not naming them all.

For my son, Gershom Kean Bazerman, bright star

THE PACIFIC BETWEEN

Scavenging
(Whidbey Island)

Scavenging on Double Bluff

1.
My children call these wish-stones, Anne said,
Studying the warm brown quartz
I had picked with its perfect elongated
White circle; when that circle is
Unbroken, that's what makes them wishes.
I wished she had not told me this.
All week I thought of getting another
Down by Double Bluff Beach.
This afternoon I take the time to bike
And walk. Some of us can pick unbroken
Spindles where others see only fragments
And shell bits; can gather a dozen
In a minute whole and bleached.
Rocks lie everywhere on mud flats.
Serpentine, granite, sandstone, calcite,
Agate: igneous and sedimentary,
Names enough to fill my pockets.
I find the colors, lines, and shapes
As I find spindles in the shore litter.
Starving at six makes one grow up sharp
At scavenging, and I have seen
Strangers turn dubious at my luck.
My eyes stoop to the search.
I do not stop for the blue herons
Or the far islands and inlets. The heron
Hunts with me, hour after hour,
Although I no longer know what it is
I wish for: love, money, position,
Picked up like these shells and stones
That weigh down my backpack.

2.
The Chinese, as I found in Shanghai
At the garden of the Minor Administrator,
Prefer edges of unequally worn stone,

Spying buttes, peaks, and scarps lift up
Against centuries. I must have never
Been Chinese. I like my rocks smooth and worn
Through millennia of storm and tide.
Round as the round of loaves; circles
Of breasts hurting with milk
On round pillows; as a lunar month finds
An open Oh! a yellow wheel;
Round scrotum swollen at touch.
Complete as unbroken bands
Of color, stones that are wishes.
I scavenge dandelion leaves, chicory,
Wild onions, beach plums, thimbleberries.
I'm scavenging in case of a famine,
Wishes worn smooth, worn daily,
In my round mouth, my anxious hand.

Seaweeds
(Puget Sound)

This is the furthest out in the Sound I'll ever be,
The ebb tide so low I've walked a quarter mile
Of sand flats rippling on and on like washboards
Laid end to end. The waves are puppies rolling
Over, lapping with blind eyes, so gentle
And tender you forget how large they'll grow,
How sloppy and brutal they can turn. Like gardens,
The seaweeds wash to and fro, shining clean
You could almost taste them fresh rinsed
In your mouth. As many greens as on this shore:
Lettuce green, early asparagus, dark-steamed
Artichoke, a bracken glow, as if sea
Water grows colors brighter than air.

Weeds is not what I would call these limpid grasses
And broad dulses. Sea wrack, rockweed, bulbous
And tufted, stringy, tubular, streamers,
Fungi-form, multiform, sea diversity
As lavish as on land. But I cannot walk
These flats endlessly. I must turn back
And face the new houses built to look out
To the Pacific. I have counted twelve flags
Streaming on the late August air drafts,
A thirteenth almost too small for myopic eyes
To note in the distance, and who knows how many
More, flags that flap or hang or fly, forbidding
And uniform. Seaweeds, green and brown, gripping
Onto their hold-fasts of shell and stone,
Drift slowly, wave with the incoming tide.
Today I have said goodbye to my son,
Let him go onto this shore of flags and gardens.

Fu

It's the first weekend of August, the innkeeper says,
There are no rooms to let. All the B & B's
Show No Vacancy signs out front in discreet letters.
We pay our money to enter a garden
Of rhododendrons turned to rough leaves
And dried seed, and imagine what it must have all
Looked like in April and May. I am always
Too late or too early, I think; and stand on barren
Ground long after roses and suckers have been pruned
To nubs.
           But on clear-cut alder we find
Huckleberry bushes, one after another,
Vermilion berries strung in half light,
Illuminated ripe for plunder.
The West has such plenty that deer
Will not feed on sweet tart wild huckleberries,
We say, stripping branches into the mouths
Of Wal-Mart bags, before heading for lunch
At a Chinese restaurant in Oak Harbor.
                  Where
Walls are plastered with Fu signs, brush-stroked
On red paper, raised on gold plastic. Leap
Of lines and tucked-in curves command and mind
The gods. Fortune, I know but had forgotten,
Is synonymous with happiness and luck
For Chinese in restaurants offering cheap
Plentiful food.
           In the dining area
Clashes of spatula against metal,
Dangerous sizzles of garlic, fish, and fowl.
Fu is the sesame in the bottle of oil
The cook from Hong Kong pours into his wok.
Fu the hours Monday to Sunday, a.m. to midnight.
Fu the smiles the tireless waitress serves
And has been serving for a hundred-
Fifty years in America, where we think genies
Fill bushes under fir and cedar with rubies.

Open Beach

A mild day: behind rough sand, ranked conifers
Climb the bluffs. Before me, the cold waters
Of Puget Sound shush on pebbled littoral.
I balance over driftwood. Drying corpses,
Rock crabs crisp-wither in the sun.
The weatherman had predicted rain.

Scarcely a dozen children, moms and dads
Lie or stroll about quiet as an Edward
Hopper painting. The waves converse
Briskly. I measure distances toward
And between to find my place. It's low tide.
Families stake towels and beach chairs and hide

A hundred yards from each other.
Their secrets served in furtive hampers
Are private on a public beach. Not touching
Children play two by two by the water
In skimpy suits. The waves' freedom releases,
Yet even here they can only wrestle.

Foghorns of a container ship bellow,
Trundling off the Sound toward a yellow
Sunset, across the Pacific, to Hong Kong,
Bangkok, Singapore, Manila, Hanoi, Tokyo.
All Asia where the ocean stops is shadowless
In this picture. The waves talk louder, crest

As the tide turns. Soon all will be water
Where mother packs her picnic basket, father
Buttons his shirt. I begin in criticism
And end in absorption, staring at Rainier
Rising blue and white, with the children,
Fatter than any cloud on any horizon.

Sweet-peas

I pick single sprays this morning,
White, lilac, pink, and powder blue
To form a handful of scent
Discreet as tears a grown woman
Does not shed before strangers.
It is foolish to address you,
Sweet-peas, in the second person.
Only sorrow leads to this fancy,
These old-fashioned words coming
From a different text than
What I must read today.

Yet I pick the sweet-peas, look
For a long time at their frail
Blossoms, these with three fringy
Petals overlapping, like mother,
Father, child, a trinity
That is broken. All August
I've picked sweet-peas from the fence
Where the vines reach out to me.
I'm told they must be picked
If they are to bear more flowers.
This is what ordinary people
Call nature, the integrity
Of a harvest for human culling,
Comfort from smells and colors,
Variety. It is our scabs
We must not pick. They'll never heal,
The doctor says. He knows
The nature of our bodies.
Both are nature, that which bears
And that which never heals.
We are broken by sorrow,
Something picks at us,
Like the woodpecker we hear,
Bang, bang, for its sustenance
Of little woodworms.

Burning Gold Paper
(California)

Burning Gold Paper

What is it with white people who buy
Gold funeral paper for note cards
And keepsakes, give bars of home-made soap
Gift-wrapped in gold that should have burned
For Phor Thor Kong, King of Hungry Ghosts,
On the day the unfed dead rush out
To feast on earth?
                              I leave the soap wrapped
To show it wasn't my idea; in case
Tai Su Lah, the Great Intellect, known
As King of Ghosts, feeds me to his demons
On the first day of the seventh month,
For acting like a westerner, not burning
This gold meant for ancestral spirits.

Ancestors deserve respect, and we deserve
The children we've raised in the West,
Unfilial.

          Chinatown is a dangerous
Place for Americans who see beauty
In funerary banknotes. Someone
Should tell them we Chinese
Are a clannish people, dislike having
Our beliefs made fun of. So much more
Our gods and devils.

                    Beware the child
Who saves gold paper for her use instead
Of throwing, sheaf upon flaming sheaf,
Into the conflagration, straight to hell.

Cheap Paper

This exercise book's stamped three dollars
And twenty-four cents. Add state and federal
Taxes. Someone had bought it in April,
Nineteen ninety-six. Abandoned journal,
Left behind with his teacher, seven pages
Scrawled with unmemorable writing, less
Than prose, passing for poetical.

The teacher saved the book. I write in it.
After all, a dollar translates into rupees,
Seven for a dollar, three of ringgit, twenty
Some other cash to feed a family
Of five for a day. Seventeen kyat
In Myanmar, seventy on the black market,
To the two hoeing the fields, baby

Swaddled and children scrabbling beside. Paper
Costs: arms and face. Losing face in the face
Of starving in the face of plenty. He'd purchased,
Not really meaning to use it, the syllabus
Unstudied. He'd no notion of labor
And consequence, and I a poor sort of teacher,
Unable to teach pluses and minuses.

Disappointment of 2 o'clock

The class is clanking
With cacophonous lines.
None is biting with zest
Or ringing with bright notes
Or scooting on scented
Toe shoes or murmuring
Amorous musk or hollering
Holy hymns and whirling
Dervishly to Diana
And Mercury. No one
Writes about demons and deep
Scary secrets or tear
Entrails foretelling futures.
Only a stray poem
Whispers, sometimes,
A promise, in words
Approaching timorously,
Bearing heraldic names.

I Slip the Catch

Soon as the students
Walk out of the last lecture,
I slip the catch.

Goodbye, year. Goodbye,
Tall students steering skateboards!
You, with orange hair,

Asthmatic breathing,
Goodbye! Quick ears! Steel mesh grin!
Sweet anorexic!

Bye, baby beer guts,
Nose ring and stud, dirty mind
And worser writing!

Chemists, accountants,
Traders, and salsa dancers!
Gladly we vanish.

Bless this Bagel

Bless this bagel this Sunday morning,
Stark cold, week-old, toasted crisp.
Bless this toaster humming, electricity
Zipping from pole to pole, wires that power
The flour. Bless the marmalade,
Gold with zest and peel, bitter-sweet
Like this land of oranges and sweat labor.
Bless this thick plain peanut butter
I spread, scraping excess, waging
The difference between greed and pleasure.
Bless the morning, its history
Of pleasures, its lesson of meaning
Of other meanings disappearing
In the frugal love this morning knows.

Eating Fruit

That hard green pear, one of a dozen
Snagged in the red mesh sack, has
A blotch on one pale cheek.
Tenderly I shave it off, pare
Down to clean flesh and juice.
Eat it. Soon the others will be thrown
Into the trash, too ripe, too many.
Like the onions, round as coconuts,
Grown pungent legs; tubers hairy
And spotty; and slim bananas,
Blown brown-soggy overnight.

Papayas were dollars a pound.
I ponder: why buy one, two? How many
Would be too many? I teeter
On a decision, reach for the answer.
So it goes. Cruciferous cabbages
Are not eternal, although eternal plenty's
Promised here. What is as lovely
As lemons heaped in a bowl, sunlight
Imprinted on skin? A miracle of loaves
And lemons at my hand turns daily.
Still, I do not know how to eat
For one, for two, cannot learn the lesson
Of plenty. Is beauty one or bounty?
Will these fruits, shades of gold and glop
On the plate, stay ideal and sound?

Home

It is midnight. I wake up and listen.
One is snoring next to me, heavy
With sleep and middle age. Downstairs, one
Is coughing and talking to the television.
They are what I have. I dare not ask
For more. Human love is what's at home,
Dazed and on edge. Listening at dusk
To an unknown bird, learning the task
Of naming, one at a time, in a new
Country, I acknowledge humbly,
This is all can be asked: proximity
In a carriage carrying us forward
As one through the short night hours,
To disperse when the light breaks through.

The Mourning Months

I.
Spring arrives in March in triplicate hues,
Pink, purple, lilac, the color of gray
Women's scarves, variable shades of magnolia

Afloat on branches or petals loose
On grass. I tie my sneakers—over
Sixty, out for my morning walk, Dorothy

To eye more months. In June and July
The year will be blue jacaranda
Lining Cathedral Oaks, blue hydrangea
Swollen, drenched in circling sprays.

II.
Today the vibrant peach buds poke
Open, vulgar as those Stepmother embroidered

In the years after Father brought her home.

I was six years younger, she a mother
Swelling with babies. We never spoke,
Nor has she ever seen a real peach blossom.

III.
Man is in love and loves what must die,
As do women. The Indian Night Jasmine
Ripens the Santa Barbara sky

With Sicilian-born mustard seed
And African tulip trees. I pace
Past day lilies that look somewhat

Like Wordsworth's daffodils, yellow as
Morning sunshine, bred and plotted
In fenced yards. Yellow, like California

Wood sorrel thick sprouted beside
Pacific beaches, like black mustard's
Citrus clusters sluggish with heavy bees.

Allergic in a new country, I am running
Against months, choking on the everyday
Pollen of nature, not daring, carrying
The years' exiled austerities.

Memory Loss

There are few winters in Santa Barbara,
Only sun, blue skies, creamy surf most days.
A newcomer wonders, who works where
Nature's so lavish it seems unnatural
To remain mournful? I'm at a loss here,
Loosening my grip on yesterday.
Should I continue in this vein I will lose
Shades of father and mother, shadows
Of images in negatives that silvered
The poem as I knew her. Should I continue
In this sunshine she will bleach into
A handkerchief page for no tears, good
For no poetry, if what the sunny blue
Days say is also what she can say.

California Disaster

First time I felt an earthquake I did not know
To be afraid. Curious, feeling for the first time
Myself a still center while the ground swayed
And things shimmered like I'd shimmered all my life.
How queer to be still, body alert as if
In a nightmare. The silverware was rattling
Like a Gatling machine-gun in its drawer,
And the crockery ground against each other
As if a maddened maid had jangled the plates
And soup bowls with her thrashing hands,
Just as I'd often wished to do in this kitchen
Of my dreams. The jams and spice bottles on top
Of the refrigerator tapped and danced
In defiance of common sense. I thought
What made the house unsteady was
My alter ego out with a vengeance,
Shaking the heavy frames, impatient
Of the value of pictures held in four
Corners. Strange how angry I'd been for years
In the country of my dreams, uncracked, locked in.
Then the jitters stopped, and I forgot
What I'd glimpsed.
                          The second time the rolling
Was so strong and long, asleep, I knew
It wasn't the body shuddering but the ground.
The books came down from their half-hearted shelving,
The low coffee table leapt askew,
Someone died, the radio said, and a few more
Later. This was life, mortifying, books
And table returned to tableaux, dust and ash
On old loves wiped away, like heirlooms
When quakes and their fires jolt and char
That, packing the car, evacuating,
We'd have left behind with no remembrance.

Past Danger and Drowning
(Newcastle, Australia)

Past Danger and Drowning
(Newcastle, Australia)

Mornings I set off for the Pacific,
Her heaving bosom stretched between
Rivals gazing from opposite shores.
Silicate, shell, and stone roil beneath her touch,
Back and forth, groaning, while she slips
Away and toward suns rising
And setting, and the surfer men come daily.

I also adore her, threaded to her fine
Eyebrow horizons. Shadowed swells raise
My thirst no matter how much I swallow.
I can never be a woman like her,
Forever wet, incipiently
Violent, even when calmed. In Newcastle
Young boys and older throw their bodies
Passionately at her each morning,

Naked male skin carried toward dark rock
And cars. By sides of streets they strip,
Wriggle into work-clothes, and day
Collapses into schools, offices, coal-mines
And their women's arms, awake and sullen
In the world of dry air. They are mermen,
Stolen away from their mothers' hips.
And I? Drawn early down to Bogie Hole,

Treading the slippery convict-shattered
Stone steps, descend to the maddened
Slamming of her spittle against boulders,
Gulp the white and yellow sprays that break
In digital seconds never returning.
Like our men moving on to other bodies,
While the ocean woman breathes out, breathes in,
Cradling her surfers past danger and drowning.

Bogie Hole

Before that old crone curse, arthritis,
Comes down on me, I walk up Newcastle Beach
To Bogie Hole. What power, I ask, peering
Over the handrails at the sea-moss
Slime-slippery steps cut into the cliff face
Steep down to rock hold, studying
As if a text the heart skips over,
Falling in love with falling, before
Backing off from the salt savor.
Not yet, feet say, stepping away.

Today for the first time I see dolphins
Jumping above the surf line, black fins
Racing over the Pacific, natural
As feet walking in sunshine on Bathers' Way.
What has brought me to Newcastle no one
Knows, least of all me. Blue skies and ocean air
The same as home, leaving home is mere practice
For leaving all, all the leavings learned
Again and again, until goodbye becomes
Addictive, last look behind, first look forward,
What you carry everywhere. What childhood taught,
Packing up, sleeping on others' mattresses,
Always hungry for the new morning
And night to be endured, sharp as a knife
Peeling another brown spot.

Nobby's Beach

I see him hobble on one long strong leg,
The other a dangling stump, third a crutch,
In swimming shorts and tee, and sit
On the wood-slatted bench near the parking lot
And sucking surf hot distant meters away.
He says this sandy stretch, Newcastle's boast,
Appears like acres of tears he hadn't shed
When they lifted him out of Shark Alley
Winters ago, after the juvenile gray snagged
The limb from him. Harder to cross with hobble,
Crutch, and one good leg than you'd imagine.

Afternoons between lunch and sunset crowds
He sits watching black-suited amphibian boys
Hurry with bee-waxed boards into the waves
Like elegant seals in and out of ocean,
Ignore his gaze that says nothing except
Wonder where among the watery particles
His flesh and blood now surge with the spindrift
And its tide, sensations of thigh and calf
And foot and toes clasping like that bite
Still threshing its fish head in the surf
Most afternoons on Nobby's Beach.

WALKING BACKWARDS

Passport
(Hong Kong)

Passport

Having arrived now
            At the celestial kingdom,
I do not enter.

I am walking backwards into China
        Where everyone looks like me
And no one is astonished my passport
        Declares I am foreign, only
Envious at my good luck. Speechless,
        Without a tongue of China,
I remember Grandfather's hands, Grandma's
        Tears. On Causeway Bay, ten thousand
Cousins walk beside me, a hundred
        Thousand brothers and sisters.

The Source

China is the source I have not studied,
Although she/he has been a constant
Like mother, father in memory.
China was the milk that was too heavy,
That made one gag. Vomit. Like the scent
Of stinky tofu. Temple bonzes
Muttered no books of instruction.
Women taught other women what
Was right and wrong, and they were almost
Always wrong. Center of the world, great lump
Of decay where no one is happy,
Was China in Malacca, a misfit, dumb
Country; and I its misfit child,
Bastard and deaf, handicapped and wild.

Marble and Peonies

Two hundred and sixty green peaks and stones
Floating over a vaporous sea:
This is the scene poets and painters
Make much of in the classical tradition.
Junks, lighters, and big ships like minor
Islands adrift, and the silver sheen
Of morning light on the open water
Of the South China Sea. Distance saves us
From reality, and the mysterious
Becomes a luxury we can envy.
Down on the ground, bus drivers lurch
Their stick shifts toward Central's towers,
And the cursing ferrymen
Are casting off the cable ropes as
Everyone seems to be traveling
From bed to work, from island to island.
Close up, sweat shines and sticks; no one's smiling.
The emperor loved the beauties
Of mist and distance, the corruption
Of the harem. His fringed kingdom
Wavers between ground and sky,
Decomposing marble and peonies.

Blossoming

My body is blossoming with bruises,
Red and blue, large as Hong Kong dollar coins
Or dim sum hargow dumplings. Lumps leap
Where I've been bitten. Spotted red
And blue, an open yam, at the end
Of two weeks, accident-prone, I hang on
From one to five-thirty a.m., to stare
At the bleak mists shred like raw cotton
Over Lama, Cheng Chou, and Lantau;
And the real China to the north. I am afraid
Of this China, unseen estrangement
Of strangers from whose lives I'm supposed
To make my story. How do we learn to take
Identity after identity, swallowing
Identities and history, to save us
From contagion of losses and predatory
Nations? In the city, anopheles mosquitoes
Bite, and hardness scars within, even
If I'm not thinking that something violent
Is happening somewhere out of sight,
Even as I sit here, safe, on the wrong side
Of the border.

Leaves Fall Close
(Pok Fu Lam [Lucky Mountain Trees] Park)

The reservoir is a cliché of calm
Despite its Cantonese name. Masters
And indentured agreed these were trees—
"Lam"—and mountains. Masters saw
England: mists and winds rolling down
The Peak another Lake District,
Except off the coast of China. The other
Saw China, classically brushed
In bamboo lines; and the greater China
Behind, reaching beyond the tears
Of the Yellow River all the way to Beijing.

"Lam"—Cantonese for "Lim." Ideogram
Of trees upright with thick thrusting branches.
Leaves fall close to their roots. Clichés
Surface from speechless calm,
Returning me, unspeaking,
To where I'd not known I'd been.

Bird Sonnet
(Pok Fu Lam Reservoir)

Butterfly season. Purple, green, and blue blurs:
Spectral light, humming birds hovering
Moments into a launch above gyrating
Red-gold dragonflies. Planetary visitants
Like us. Dragonflies adore water the way
Women are greedy for love, buzzing
Among the reservoir's collection ponds.
Putrid waters where lost and dead things
Drift, and rushing down, drains of yesterday's
Monsoon. Their wings mount wet air
Toward nectar pools in wildflower calyxes:
Time already past, glimpsed in May's
Green colors, variegated lapidaries
And grains, wavering flight and fleetness.

Resolution and Retirement

I.

I go to hunt a poem this Sunday,
Perhaps find a friend, young, thinner,
Eager for prizes and Monday.
Minutes up the mount before the gate,
My thighs ache and my chest's constricted.
I have never learned to slow down, simply
Stopped, felled by cough and fever.

II.

Mothers stroll the path, feeding solitary
Sons pastries and idle conversation.
The little walk by the pump-house is littered
With fresh dog shit drying immaculately
Under the December sun. At water's edge
Something splashes—a carp, duck, turtle,
Released by Taoist priests who come at noon
To free the captured ghosts who swirl by
Mongkok's frenzied alleys. Bodies tortured
By triads, crying in their families' nightmares.
It's time for me to become a lady
Of leisure, freed from officious spirits.

III.

Tall grasses bend toward the North Star
Even when the air is calm. One cannot resist
The mountain's influence: the way water
And wind flow in relation to season,
Its feng shui. Here where the foam spills
In falls over the collection grates,
Someone is wearing a Stanford T-shirt.
I cannot stay satirical.
The morning's cool and bright. Why should I
Not walk beside wild rhododendron,

Bamboo, giant mimosas flat open
To sunbeams, breeze-blown air rippled
With plash of hidden streams and children's
Cantonese, high-pitched, musical, and be content?

City Pastoral

Night is over. CNN is on.
Red and yellow taxis, tops lit
Like go-go girls, prowl the macadam.
Above, in the brightening heaven,
Engines crank. No angels are dusting.
Only the island smog shifts
With sleepers on doorsills.

Last night in Causeway some were fucked
For power, peace, money, love.
Mongkok grandmas sold shoes and wallets.
Uncles were swindled. Some fathers' luck
Came in, ran out. Minibuses sped
With panting breaths, brown stinking coughs,
Condemned, necessary and crammed.

Across the hotel's scythe-shaped window
Serial towers of glowing slate rise
Empty of people. White drawn glass crowd
With drying shirts, frayed towels, gray
And riotous underwear; kettles, pots,
The what-may-have-you despised
That citizens cannot live without.

The happy weatherman is getting back
To us on his little prison screen,
Just as the April sun has risen ever
Higher, ruthless, above the gun-black
Windows. Just, as everywhere, a child
Is waking, fresh, clear-eyed, clean,
Ready for joy in the smoky city fields.

Your First Birthday
(For a Chinese Matriarch)

The first birthday you as a Chinese
Woman can have is when you turn sixty.
Everything before is not worth thinking of
Or can bear remembrance. Sixty is when
You become human: you, a person
Fortunate enough to live so long
The children, villagers, even the Emperor
Will congratulate you.

                    Most died before sixty:
Hunger, beatings, coughing diseases,
Waste, hanging, or simple sorrow
That turns their faces to the wall and calls
Forth death to sit on their chests
And smother their miserable breath.

But sixty, when the hair is thinner and ash-gray
Combed into your curls reminds you of where
Even your hard knucklebones must go,
You may sip to these years with French brandy,
Red ginseng, rare hot ginger, and the blood
Of fowl. Hens that still lay, young roosters
Crowing with semen. Everything that's full
Of life—to be slaughtered for you,
Should you survive life's slaughtering.
At sixty you may drink all the blood
You can stomach, having become an eater
Of young, a human, on your first birthday.

Seminar Series
(Hong Kong University, 5 p.m., Thursdays)

Listening to a very important person
                read his seminar paper
                      we all fell
into a trance
like passengers on a long
          and tedious train ride
              during which everyone was afraid
to fall asleep
in case the fascist
        commandant threw you
                out of the window,
staying awake to save our lives,
as the professor train steadily
             moves along the
                  indistinguishable
anonymous tracks
going nowhere
        into a twilight darker
              and darker into night.

Hong Kong Muses

I.
My bed floats above the ship's horn,
A long bass note waking me
At 3:30 dawn, a little after
Fitzgerald's dark night. To my right
The air purifier blows steadily.
Steady the reading light by my side.
It's not cracked fame makes me linger,
Or the thrum of the mighty city
Running on wheels and ferries outside
The high windows from where I'd studied
The dirty sun sink to the western sea.
Something wants to be said, has thrown
Its mazy colors with this earliest hour,
In signs foreign and my own.

II.
She comes from a place I hardly remember
To taunt: Amazon, Boddicea,
Queen of the Night, with her coven, dark hair
Sprinkling shampooed sparks and spite, stalker
Of boys and victories. I catch her cloudy
Figure moving ahead. Mistral, Santa Ana,
Hamadan: parting the future, freezing
The waters of the past. Who needs the other more?
The white crane or the shadow-boxer?
I long for the easy life of women herding
Calves and sheep toward fat pastures.
Lead me not into temptation, I write,
Even as she rushes past me, pulling
Walls down, and suspends all, in transit.

III.
Betraying no one but my self,
Music sings loud and louder,
Filling the hours between speaking
And sleep. Among the young
This morning I treaded water,
Floating on airs. Tonight,
An old woman, am led by music
Whose voice suffuses then falls,
A tempo that slips away,
Like you, memory, measured
And immeasurable, betraying
No one but my self.

IV.
Every night she screams, doors slam,
Her dogs bark in the flat below.
Ship-horns blow slow bass space
Resounding thick requiems.

Listening I try to sleep.
No one is here but me, sad, yet not
Unhappy. The woman a floor
Below has fallen silent. Deep

Quiet presses with the cold
Slow rolling down the Peak.
Awake again I know it's time
To quit, for home and the world.

Two Years

Two years is a long digression.
In the meantime I have learned
A new city, although only partly.
Have failed to learn a new language,
Merely words and phrases.
Made a few friends, a number
Of enemies. Have thought hard about
Where I am going. Lost.
And where I want to go. Home.

The islands still rise above
The South China Sea. I will never
Explore more than three or four.
China bulks forbidding
Although no longer forbidden.
Sick of excessive humankind,
Sicker of colonial adventurers
Who fatten on Asian taxes,
I think of Li Po, light a candle, and write.

Feng Shui
(Homeground)

Feng Shui

> "Make your heart small."
> Chinese proverb for girl-children

Wind and mountain, wave and rock: Tua Ehm,
First Uncle's hard-headed wife, said bad feng shui
Did us in. The door opening to a T-road
To thieving peddlers, beggars, and children.
The missing mirror in which demons
Of strangers could have been plucked
And scared away. Such was the luck
I had never learned, to make the entrance
Crooked, my feet bound, and heart
Small. I have walked away from Chinese
Fortune-telling. Crossed the big water,
Married a big nose. Now my American house
Is empty of children. It too will part
In pockets of ghosts, hosted by strangers.

Hunger Verses

1.
Thinking is easy when all you need
For happiness is a bowl of noodles.

2.
Father rides his old bike
To work every morning.
Rides back in the burning
Late afternoon sun. Has he
Dollars in his pocket?
Will we eat tonight?

3.
Sour pickled cabbage—
Hard green yellow lumps,
Salted, months old,
From faraway Fujian
To the wet market
Beside the dirty river
On to our plank table.
Delicious.

Generations and History

Dat's why I neber go back church.
Ebeywon say Asians silent type.
They no meet my mudder.
She nebber stop talking
like Asian suppos to be.
They suppos to keep bad feeling
inside, they hurt and truble feeling.
Not all mem'ry of war,
beating brudder and sista.
All terr'ble story all shut inside.
I wish my mudder not do dat,
talking and talking all day, eben at night.
I wish she shuddup. No mo pain
for me, all happy happy like.
Not like church where ebeyone,
eben the minister say,
Hallejuah sista, shout it out.
I no wan shout out terr'ble story.
I no wan hear no more.

KEEPING YOUR DISTANCE

For My Mother

I sent a letter
careful to say
nothing
to hurt
I sent a check
thinking, that's all
she'll want
because I knew
there was more
she wanted
I sent some photos—
See, here I am
sitting, standing
you can put me
in your pocketbook
in the pages
of your Bible.

A different daughter,
or mother,
would surely
have shared
a life
of common happiness.

How convenient
to be so busy:
chores and papers
meetings talks
washing up cleaning
hemming days
in stitches, all tucks,
no ruffles,
and late at night
another day
gone to seed,
unborne.

Letter from Abroad

My fingers
feel the letters—
H u s b a n d.
Conjure his image, rough.
Scrubby.
Good solid land
for settling, ground
to husband.
Gratitude's
like milk-weed
found between stones,
hospitable dirt.
Sends rootlets
to draw what need
nourishing. Fortitude
magnified
by small perspective.
Feeds the butterflies,
has fed both us
and me.
I close eyes,
feel through fingers:
this is to husband.

Six Ages

I.
I found a poem
in the diaper pail.
It wasn't running
like egg-yolk, or cheesy
and green curdled.
But it was no good
anyway dropped
among the fouled
diapers, and baby
kicked his feet and cried
to be changed
one more time.

II.
A poet drove us down, pink with pleasure,
to his island. On the dirty launch,
lunchless, I held you firmly above
the oily sea. You would have eluded
my hand to fall seal-like, drifting
from my gaze into the murky salt.
Mournful, I grasped you through the engine
smoke and swirling water an hour long,
until the brown mossy bottoms
of glittery white coral saved us.
So mothers remember death in their love,
hold tight in the whirl of transformed atoms
the lively infant who squirms with seas
and worms, loathing another's form.

III.
The volcanoes lock in the islands,
thigh-ridged, fibrous. Every hour
buses run from our bungalow
to Waikiki. We wait in the sun.
You read Captain America comics,

while I concentrate on salt-licking
Pacific wave-on-wave rocking.
The grass mat dries to a stiff shroud.
In my ears tongues of breezes
pulse steady sibilants.

At the Vietnamese restaurant you eat
diced pork, whole branches of basil
wrapped in fraying rice paper.
Will you remember to write this
for the third grade teacher, I ask,
What I did for summer vacation?
The skewed joy of eating paper
twists in your comic-book eyes.
But even as you grin huge gaping
ungrown teeth, I know
you will already have forgotten it.

IV.
The door bangs, shoes scuff, and the house is full
of you. For a minute the day unfrowns
its work, and generations settle down
to a shuffle. You were a fat mouth
that morning home from hospital.
Fancy footwork at one, falling and reeling.
But thirteen is too grown for crying,
too old for mothers. Schooling and facts,
you're superior to a sofa, to kitchens
and maids. The humming blue screen
takes you in for hours, sitting god-wise;
emerge, another day, removed, cleansed
of human voice. Within machines
you wait for whatever is coming with your sunrise.

V.
This child who smiles from within four
corners of a photograph embraces
the rough bark of a tree at a forgotten
park in a moment like the thumbprint

of an illiterate swearing earnest money
for the bearer. Even now, seventeen years
later, two scarlet insect bites scar
the chubby arm that clings unselfconscious
to the trunk, immediate and near
as his milk teeth unevenly grown.

Calcium returned to earth. No scab remains.
Only this round-cheeked photo propped between
audiotapes and cd's, a Grecian urn
Bright after-vision in a general
blankness. Justice of a sort, I suppose,
generation after generation
disappearing at each end. A stranger posed
tall, rough as that trunk on which the child
rests his cheek, is vanishing. Coming behind,
motherhood stops, Eve is fallen.

VI.
You no longer will sit across from me.
Something in you shuns me.
Shuns my face, my breasts, my arms.
The same that made you love me
when you beat your wooden spoon
on a makeshift table, lord of kitchen
and my days, is the same that drives you,
out, out of my house from sight of me.

Keeping Your Distance

Keeping your distance is what you do best,
Although it is also what I totally
Cannot do. But I am trying, I am
Trying. Distance is what the needle shows
As the car runs and runs, eating up miles
Like dessert; the needle, flicking at sixty,
Seventy, a straight pointing thing that jabs
Air and my heart—breaking down from carb
Overload and the stress of this learning.
I am learning what Americans do so well—
Staying out of each other's hair, far far
Away, not even a voice on the voicemail,
Mail reduced to e's and digital flashes
Like the flashing of turn signals. I am
Turning sixty soon myself, like the engine
Revving past Highway 101 speed limits,
Past the brute Pacific, its blue and marine life
Hidden under the blanket of sunlight
On my left. You are America, sweet
Brown grapeland, alien mustard seed, transplanted
Europe and Asia, cultivated,
Wild, exotic, as native here as almost
Anything—like me, like me. The needle
Points homeward, keeping count of distances
Traveled, we two on separate roads.
This land produces the story I am telling you.

Exile's London

A soft-edged city, circled by Cupolas,
Parks, Needles, and lindens' gray shooters.
A Pakistani family strolls by,
Mother's trousers flowering in eggplant silk.
Bells from the famous church clamor
Nine o'clock. Everyone is carrying
An overnight bag. I slacken, gaze
At the green sunny grass and darker
Green canvas chairs as if into *A Child's
Book of London*. It's Sunday.
Butts lie benign on pavements. Strangers
Stare possessively at that which
Is vanishing. Slip off their dusty exile
For the sensational dress of another country.

Green Parakeets

(Hofgarten, Innsbruck)

Two men in gray and brown suits stand in a halo
Of green parakeets, three perched on shoulders,
Three on extended arms, others with wingspans
Whirring in an emerald nimbus. Birds
Fly from wrists to beech trees, from branches
To arms crooked like a gentleman's
For their grace. The men are stiff and tender
And look at no one. A third lover
Splits a bright green apple and squinting ties
Both halves onto a tree. Crimson beaks
Crack rich fat peanuts, let them fall
Where dozens and dozens of blue serge pigeons
Clamber underfoot. The Tyrols rise
On one side, snow-screened European cones
On this November morning. The bleak
Night is over, the train-ride from Vienna
Awake toward a nameless hotel
Done. I am struck by these tropical beauties,
Their gentle handling, and the old men
Who do not smile but look away.
A moment before, walking alone and slowly,
I had loosed the breath held in hurry,
Stepping into the scene of green-fed parakeets
In this chilly Austrian park, like the mothers
Pushing strollers and matrons groomed for their walk.
The men in loden suits straight as pensioned
Soldiers looking sternly away from me
Remind I am straying before the mind
Of Europe and breathless I must travel
From the green birds, green apple, and their mountains.

Woman Traveling
(Katmandu)

Coming down from Manakamana, temple of the wish-fulfilling
goddess, our bus stinks of goat. The young kid is silent, tired
after its trek in the cable car across the flank of the Himalayas to
her ancient courtyards, slipping on gore, past headless creatures
twitching and dead. Pilgrims feed solemn children coconut shreds,
peanuts, tangerines peeled with bloodstained fingers. I hope
sacrifice is a figure of speech, the dazed goat to be ferried home
and petted.

We stop to reconnoiter, scramble down a riverbank to a sandy
beach by Trisuli, flowing clear and deep toward India. The
headmaster's knife must have slit its throat. I do not look yet see
it struggle while men circle, bowls held to catch the bright arterial
gush to set to puddings. As in childhood dreams, nothing is
wasted, liver and heart wrapped in leaves, fried with onions, silvery
glistening innards uncoiled washed in the stream rushing down,
bearing a dead rat and where the children shit.

This is how the middle class feasts in Nepal when the goddess
protects from harm and the evil eye: boiling a cauldron full of
whitest rice, an iron pot of curried goat stew, kettle of churning
chai. Men eat and walk about. Women in festive red serve, eat last,
and more. Wash dishes as if in their kitchens.

Children from the shacks above come down and watch us eat.
Bare feet, bare bottoms, they cartwheel, chase, and laugh, limbs
brimming while we squat and chew, old toads blinking at
dragonflies we know will be dead tomorrow. I give my plastic bags
to three to stuff with goat and rice. Others crowd in, silent, swallow
fistfuls of slop. Quick, quick, hands ball rice into mouths until
no more can enter. Then appears a small man in khaki, a green
hat signaling he's somebody, to fill his pot with leftovers: masses
remaining, a hard dark stratum I'd gladly eaten when I had wanted
rice and rice and more rice to fill me. That was a life away and

past. No longer Asian I am free to move either way: honored by men, dishonored traveler without father, husband, or brother. Pity and envy shadow the bus as it rushes to Katmandu, rattling with women's gossip and empty cauldrons.

Sometime
(after William Stafford)

Sometime when the clock is striking, ask me
If the day passed is my life. Ask me what
Schedules have ruled, why sacrifice was
Not a word I'd used, and if I have changed
My mind. Ask me who had run with the watch-
Men, who stayed, then ask me where I'd lived
And why. We will stop to listen
To the clock's clamor, its continuous
Chatting. Squat as a toad, man-made
And mechanical, screws and springs
Denoting neither eternity nor
Place, it too has its core of meaning,
Second to second, explaining nothing.
What the clock says, that is what I say.

No Place

Touching down, I've touched a nerve from another life. Everywhere is new and strange-familiar when there is nothing to return to. Every house mine, every street my street, every man my husband, every place the last place I'd lived in. I'd never thought this lingering question odd. Why not? I could have been the waitress in Paris, bored, weary of summer as she serves. Or the New Delhi matron, wondering, is it jasmine sprays or marigold punk she smells between bites of naan? An English woman asking for tea and telly. Amnesiac, I sight ordinary inhabitants: not my own oneiric self, settling with no memory, an immigrant story.

Solitary
(Cambridge, Massachusetts)

The leaves are falling, yellow, copper, dun.
Days falling one by one into November,
December. Another year's done.

Winds stir the high gingko branches. A glass
Seats me beside their twirling leaves.
Below, spendthrift lies gold on grass.

Only a wall separates me from the bullying cold.
My red jacket hangs by a nail. It is too soon
To be up and walking, to wrap and fold

Myself against the Boston air. Too late
To begin singing lessons.
Life was too busy. Too busy every date.

Yesterday was blue and golden. Today it rains.
It rains. What rains? The sodden clouds
Wrung wet. Air itself. Eyes' imaginings.

This hour slides inside a stranger's room
With other hours, other fictions.
Here are tides. Here the rising moon.

Changing Gears

It's 2:30 a.m. and it dawns on me
I am changing gears like the quiet
Spanish town five floors below. It's three

Years since I've been back in Pamplona,
A blip in a life, the seconds-hand
Where I hold the watch ticking below

My chin in the darkness to guess
At the hour. Of course it's too early,
Too early, a waste of time, time wasted.

I'm cold although the room is warm,
Cold inside, not unhappy; cold alone,
Not miserable. There is no harm,

I am not unhappy waking
Alone in a strange town. There is nothing
Wrong with drift although drifting

Is terrifying, drifting while the great
Shark above widens its jaws.
It is guttural, the insipid grind

Of its triple row of teeth. You
Cannot dodge the teeth, not that insipidity
Can be avoided. A killer of hours who

Flashes darkness and brilliance,
Cleverness itself yawning.
Is this what being is about? The lances

Of the gears like the teeth of the shark
Grind and mesh. Both are and eat me,
Finally understanding nothing dark

Separates the stupid and the clever,
Understanding the shine of teeth
Looming above the beloved head of summer.

After Forever

Every morning I go walking,
And every afternoon also.
Stained dark wood, burned,
As I was a half century and more ago
Under an equatorial sun,
Walking unfed, ill-clad,
Determined, without a sense
Of determining what I wanted.

Somewhere along the way
I dropped forever off
Like a bag of kitchen waste
On the side of the Taconic Parkway.
Without a guilty pang,
A cheapskate homeowner
Who won't pay for garbage collecting
And cruises every Thursday
For a spot to throw out the rotting
Peels of the week, fish bones,
And scraps of roast.

Like an immigrant
Stopping to sit curbside,
Trunk filled with clothing
Five sizes too small, saved
For decades while she waits to shrink
Back to size, to return
To someone else's residence, that first home
Of the child's hand-me-down dress,
Waiting then to devour
The apple of this sunlit world,
The scene after forever.
When did I give up forever
For the slow walk and goodbye,
Steps pacing a street in late afternoon?

The Good Soldier

His face lies flat on the newsprint,
Gazes out of the death frame.
Cut jaw, clenched gaze, hint
Of adventure ahead--clarified
By our blunt knowledge no fresher image
Will return our reading or reply.
Day after day nothing changes but the name:
Armstrong, Rodriguez, Sawyer, Nguyen.
And years: seventeen and thirty-three,
Fifty-one and twenty-six. This age my son's,
These features another mother's gladness.
I gaze to fix meaning to shape,
Iraq to America. Tweak out of grey
Newspaper the honor it declares.
Stumped by two-dimensional faces,
Brother, father, husband, son; some already
Orphaned, some fearing blown, flattened
On yesterday's papers. He, and she,
Good soldiers, marching past posts in past tense.

Writing a Poem

The air is buzzing. Some one near by
is operating a giant machine. He's scrubbing
a just sold building with a high-
powered hose. None of us are listening,

although we are each hopeless before
this dizz-dizz-dizz. If it was a monstrous
radiated beetle, we couldn't be more
helpless. It's eating up the hours

as if they were the sweet nectar of day,
which they are. It is impossible
to think or write. Its buzz takes away
feelings, takes over ears, is drilling a hole

in a loose tooth as you sit in history's
dental chair, frantic and still, the drill
hammering the gums until only
spit oozes, dribbles, spills over, fills

cavities you didn't know you had,
only the drill lives in your head
only the dull sharp dizz-dizz-dizz.
This is how the poem ends, dizz-dizz. . . .

On Why I Continue To Write Poetry
(for Adrienne Rich)

I think of Anna Akhmatova,
grieving, awkward,
writing on cigarette paper,
toilet paper, the backs
of bills and envelopes,
in her mind, at night, when
it's a blackout, when she knows
there are watchers
at her window. Writing
in her ear, her voice,
on skin, her body a sheet
of paper for words she cannot
put down. Carrying her fear,
love, hatred, those words
written down on her life.
She's nobody, a woman
without a husband, they'd
shot him at midnight,
and she cannot cry yet.
But see, here are her poems,
here is her cry
fifty years later,
a hundred years later
Anna Akhmatova
is still writing,
and Stalin is dead.

Metaphor

Dream is
a metaphor for life
lived underground.

Empty-handed
poetry comes
with empty pockets.

The dog barks
after midnight although there are
no burglars.

The sheriff and his wife
demanded
a pound of flesh.

I said I was sorry,
I wasn't thinking when I took her
bicycle for a ride.

A Curious Book

A curious book is a woman,
crooked neck tucked into
a book. It reads like a woman
reading—her life a library
stacked and restacked. A woman's
like a book she reads, frowning.

Freedom Day

Having bought the story of responsibility I now try to change it at the warehouse for a better story. The warehouse has only outdated, defective, and very expensive stories in stock. I go up and down the aisles. Nothing works. Each falls apart just as I pick it up and turn on its engine. Many bear labels saying, Made in Greece, Italy, Britain, United States of America. It doesn't matter. Those made in China, Japan, Malaysia and Singapore are also rusting. Their engines sputter instead of roar. Small parts rattle, fall out like broken twigs. Aisles radiate all around seeming to lead everywhere. I am growing tired. The small high windows are streaked with cobwebs, partially covered by more boxes full of old stories. What should I do now?

Love Poem

I.
I am incapable of an honest
love poem, not being an honest
woman. Therefore let us read
dishonest poems, of love, of hate,
trying to get along
    shifty-eyed and hurting
    fearful and unhappy.

II.
He wrote an un-ironic love poem
to fly through absence. The irony
of love: nowhere truer
than where it addresses itself,
itself—lover absent—nowhere truer.

The Ex-Lover

"People could never talk coherently about ex-lovers,
not for fifty years. . . ."

Leslie Marmon Silko, *Almanac of the Dead* (143)

One day you start walking away without
realizing that's what you're doing. Even
as you say I love you and beg for one
more smile, you have gone down the road
and out of sight. He thinks he's the one
you live for, but it's months since you've left.
The hot steamy wind in your mouth you
swallow with your goodbye tastes like life
itself—bright, hopeful, scary life you
run toward, better than love and its
miserliness.
   Or so she thinks, shrink-wrapping
the present in its past, the man in paper,
carrying him like a paperback on the shuttle
to another airport, another meeting.

Late

My thoughts beat like the strings of the pipa
vibrating in butterfly wings.

Oh to be the courtesan whose fingers
pick your body so skillfully
you beg to be robbed again and again.

Speaking slowly your words thrum in me
until I must get up and dance
to the sounds of rain that fill
the room and overflow my senses.

Holding your memory
holding the sky,
one by one the stars
wink and blaze.

Three August Poems

I. Compassion

I won't write this poem.
It will get no attention
from that heartless
caretaker who takes all
and throws it all away.
No, I'll not give him
the satisfaction,
chucking out a hard-won
poem. I'll just strangle
it mewing in its cradle,
and sit in silence
all day.

II. Wasting

Wasting a morning, I walk to the library,
opened despite the economic downturn,
furloughs, and recession. Folks are leaving town
every month, every day, bills unpaid,
rents overdue. Or dying, strapped to beds,
wires breathing. Landlords and landladies,
daughters and executors drop big brown bags
by the side door, books no one wants,
a planet of forests cut down, falling
out of torn-bottom bags, spilling over
with words no one wants to read.
The volunteer sticks labels on each,
a dollar or two. The enormous
color cookbooks and encyclopedias
go for three. Thirty years outdated,
they are too old, like their owners,
even for a pittance. This one for a dollar,
book of poems, is six years out,
a youngster of small prattling confessions,

minor epiphanies only
woman's eye, framed to the smallness
of her world, can love and polish:
lost luggage, nursing homes, cats
stray and at home, objects like sneakers,
cremations, houses. I'd met
the poet once—she was snooty,
annealed in fame. No one wants the poems,
perhaps not even herself.
I plunk down my lowly bill,
for the ideal of an afterlife,
for the poem, all poetry,
bursting out of any poet.

III. Daughter To None

My mother had only one daughter,
and I have none. The women
of my family are all dying

in me. One day we will be like we've
never been born. Never been here
with this light pouring from a blue

sky too bright to be called blue,
August blue in a town my mother
did not live to see, never lived to hear

named. So also with most of wisdom
and sorrow I will never live
to hear of or from. The little we two
shared of blood will fall as finite ash.

Sacrament

Who was I to say who I am?
Nobody knows, least of all me,
that secret, tight as a bud,

not opening, withered before flowering.
If I had flowered, who would I have been?
But here I am, despite everything,

flowering and withering.
Here I am, someone's flower.
The flower Me is the only story

I know how to tell.
This is not the body I chose,
scarred, fused, broken.

This is not the mouth I wanted,
pursed, drawn down like blinds
all day. This is not the heart I liked,

pulsing, uplifted in and out
of love. This is what I have and when
the day comes my eyes will be shut

by a stranger's palm. Growing older
is senseless. The body's knowing is faith
and ignorance, and time will ease

with her palm the eyes' ecstasy
in scene and blue-ware, mouth's reverence
of salt and fat, ears' exultation in voice,

skin's worship of touch, and the nose,
to the nose's rule—
memory and curry and rose—

she will say, *eternity.*